can we talk?
Conversations for Faith

STUDENT JOURNAL

by Emily J. Anderson
and
Kendy L. M. Easley

edited by Laura B. Lewis, Richard R. Osmer, and Amy S. Vaughn

©1999 Geneva Press

All rights reserved. No part of this book may be reproduced or transmitted in any form or by any means, electronic or mechanical, including photocopying, recording, or by any information storage or retrieval system, without permission in writing from the publisher. For information, address Geneva Press, 100 Witherspoon Street, Louisville, Kentucky 40202-1396.

Unless otherwise noted, scripture quotations are from the New Revised Standard Version of the Bible, copyright © 1989 by the Division of Christian Education of the National Council of the Churches of Christ in the U.S.A., and are used by permission.

The poem "Who Am I?" has been reprinted by permission from *Letters and Papers from Prison*, Dietrich Bonhoeffer, Revised, Enlarged Edition, Simon & Schuster, 1971.

Book design by Vincent Mejia
Cover design by Sharon Adams

Printed in the United States of America

Contents

Introduction 4

Created for a Purpose
What Am I Doing Here? 7

What Would You Say?
Who Is Jesus Christ? 20

Sin and Forgiveness
What Does God Expect of Me? 36

**The Holy Spirit and
a Relationship with Christ**
How Can I Know God? 46

The Church and Its Mission
If God Slept In on Sundays, Why Can't I? 57

The Sacraments and the Lord's Prayer
The Church's Toolbox 67

Developing a Rule of Life
How Does God Expect Us to Live? 85

Introduction

Think about the key people in your life—your closest friends, your parents, a significant other. How much time do you spend talking and listening to them, doing things together, or sharing meals? Those of you with long-distance friends know what a challenge it is to maintain a close friendship when you don't talk or send e-mail regularly.

As people of faith, we believe that we are created to have a relationship with God. It is our relationship with God that gives purpose and meaning to our lives, assures us that we are deeply loved, and enables us to live life to the fullest. As with all of our other relationships, our relationship with God will continue to grow and develop only if we spend time in conversation with God.

God is always with us and loves us no matter what we do. In order to grow in our faith and relationship with God, we need to pray, read the Bible, worship, think about how God is working in our lives, and listen to what God wants to say to us. This journal provides opportunities for you to do some of these things during the week. The *Can We Talk? Student Journal* will make your group sessions more fun and productive, but we hope it will also give you some new ideas for ways to spend time with God and help you to form habits of prayer and reflection in your life.

EVERY WEEK, YOU WILL FIND

The Catechism

Here you will find the catechism questions for the session, with key questions highlighted. You will use these in your group sessions, so make sure you bring your journal to each group meeting. Read them through again at home to begin your journaling time.

Reflections

This section will often focus on the catechism questions or on a reading that has been provided. Spend some time reflecting on this section each week and write down your thoughts in the space provided so that you can look back and remember what you were thinking.

Looking Ahead

Each week you will have a chance to preview the catechism questions for your next group session. You will be asked to reflect on these key questions and to choose a phrase or sentence to "hang on to." Check out the instructions in your first week of journaling for more information.

Living It Out

This section gives you an opportunity to make connections between the catechism phrase you chose to hang on to and the world you live in. Use this section to bring the catechism into conversation with your daily life.

Food for the Soul

The final section of the journal each week contains some brief passages from a variety of authors reflecting on the topic of the week. Read and reflect on these and then jot down in the margin any ideas or questions they inspire. Many of the selections are prayers–include them in your prayers to God this week.

HERE ARE SOME HELPFUL HINTS FOR MAKING THE *Can We Talk? Student Journal* WORK FOR YOU:

- Try to set aside fifteen minutes a day for prayer and reflection on the catechism or scripture verse. Setting aside the same time every day will help to make it a habit and not just something you squeeze in when you have extra time.

- Think about what is a good time for you. Are you a morning person or a night person? Do you have thirty minutes when you come home from school or just after dinner? Look for where you could best add something like this to your life and try it out for a few weeks to see if it works.

- Pick a place where you can be alone and free from such distractions as the TV, radio, and younger siblings.

- Make God a part of your conversations with the catechism and other readings each week. When you pause for reflection on the catechism questions or short readings, pray that God would be present in your thoughts. Listen for how God might be speaking to you through your readings and reflection.

- Consider forming a partnership with someone else in your group. Call each other during the week to ask how the journal is going. Make a covenant to encourage each other to stick with this discipline throughout the course and see what new habits emerge.

created for a purpose

WHAT AM I DOING HERE?

the catechism

The key questions for this session are highlighted.

Question 1. *What is God's purpose for your life?*
God wills that I should live by the grace of the Lord Jesus Christ, for the love of God, and in the communion of the Holy Spirit.

Question 2. *How do you live by the grace of the Lord Jesus Christ?*
I am not my own. I have been bought with a price. The Lord Jesus Christ loved me and gave himself for me. I entrust myself completely to his care, giving thanks each day for his wonderful goodness.

Question 3. *How do you live for the love of God?*
I love because God first loved me. Amazed by grace, I live for the Lord who died and rose again, triumphant over death, for my sake. Therefore, I take those around me to heart, especially those in need, knowing that Christ died for them no less than for me.

Question 4. *How do you live in the communion of the Holy Spirit?*
By the Holy Spirit, I am made one with the Lord Jesus Christ. I am baptized into Christ's body, the church. As a member of this community, I trust in God's Word, share in the Lord's Supper, and turn to God in prayer. As I grow in grace and knowledge, I am led to do the good works that God intends for my life.

I. THE APOSTLES' CREED

Question 5. *What does a Christian believe?*
All that is promised in the gospel. A summary is found in the Apostles' Creed, which affirms the main content of the Christian faith.

Question 6. *What is the first article of the Apostles' Creed?*
"I believe in God the Father Almighty, Maker of heaven and earth."

Question 7. *What do you believe when you confess your faith in "God the Father Almighty"?*
That God is a God of love, and that God's love is powerful beyond measure.

Question 8. *How do you understand the love and power of God?*
Through Jesus Christ. In his life of compassion, his death on the cross, and his resurrection from the dead, I see how vast is God's love for the world–a love that is ready to suffer for our sakes, yet so strong that nothing will prevail against it.

Question 9. *What comfort do you receive from this truth?*
This powerful and loving God is the one whose promises I may trust in all the circumstances of my life, and to whom I belong in life and in death.

Question 10. *Do you make this confession by yourself?*
No. With all those before me who have loved the Lord Jesus Christ, and with all who serve him on earth here and now, I confess my faith in this loving and powerful God.

Question 11. *When the creed speaks of "God the Father," does it mean that God is male?*
No. Only creatures having bodies can be either male or female. But God has no body, since by nature God is Spirit. Holy Scripture reveals God as a living God beyond all sexual distinctions. Scripture uses diverse images for God, female as well as male.

Question 12. *Why then does the creed speak of God the Father?*
Because God is identified in the New Testament as the Father of our Lord Jesus Christ.

Question 13. *When you confess God as our Father, do you mean that men should dominate women?*
No. All human beings, male or female, ought to conform their lives to the love, humility, and kindness of God. Any abuse or domination in human relationships is a direct violation of God's Fatherhood.

Question 14. *If God's love is so powerful, why is there evil in the world?*

No one can say why, for evil is a terrible mystery. Still, we know that God's triumph over evil is certain. Our Lord Jesus Christ, crucified and risen, is himself God's promise that suffering will come to an end, that death shall be no more, and that all things will be made new.

Question 15. *What do you believe when you say that God is "Maker of heaven and earth"?*

First, that God called heaven and earth, with all that is in them, into being out of nothing. Second, that God rules and supports the creation in perfect wisdom, according to God's eternal purpose.

Question 16. *Did God need to make the world?*

No. God would still be God even if heaven and earth had never been made.

Question 17. *Why, then, did God create the world?*

God's creation of the world was an act of grace. God granted existence to the world simply in order to bless it. God created the world to reveal God's glory, to share the love and freedom at the heart of God's being, and to give us eternal life in fellowship with God.

Question 18. *Does your confession of God as Creator contradict the findings of modern science?*

No. Natural science has much to teach us about the particular mechanisms of nature, but it is not equipped to answer questions about ultimate reality. Nothing basic to the Christian faith contradicts the findings of modern science, nor does anything essential to modern science contradict the Christian faith.

Question 19. *What does it mean to say that human beings are created in the image of God?*

God created us to live together in love and freedom—with God, with one another, and with the world. We are created to be loving companions of others so that something of God's goodness may be reflected in our lives.

Question 20. *What does our creation in God's image reflect about God?*

Our being created for loving relationships is a reflection of the Holy Trinity. In the mystery of the one God, the three divine persons—Father, Son, and Holy Spirit—live eternally in perfect love and freedom.

Question 21. *What does our creation in God's image say about our responsibility for the earth?*

We are responsible for seeing that the earth's gifts are used fairly and wisely. We must take care that no creature suffers from the abuse of what we are given, and that future generations may continue to enjoy the earth's abundance in praise to God.

Question 22. *What is God's providence?*

God not only preserves the world, but also continually rules over it. God cares for every creature and brings good out of evil, so that nothing evil is permitted to occur that God does not bend finally to the good.

Question 23. *What comfort do you receive by trusting in God's providence?*

The eternal Father of our Lord Jesus Christ watches over me each day of my life, blessing and guiding me wherever I may be. God strengthens me when I am faithful, comforts me when I am discouraged or sorrowful, raises me up if I fall, and brings me at last to eternal life.

reflections

Dietrich Bonhoeffer, who wrote the following poem, was a pastor in Germany during Hitler's rise to power in the 1930s and 40s. The Nazis finally executed him in 1944, shortly after this poem was written, for his refusal to compromise his Christian faith and the way he believed the Gospel compelled him to live and act. Bonhoeffer, like all of us, felt the tension between what others see and what we know ourselves to be. Yet, in the end, it is God who created us, knows us, and uses us for a purpose.

Who Am I?

Who am I? They often tell me
I would step from my cell's confinement
calmly, cheerfully, firmly,
like a squire from his country-house.

Who am I? They often tell me
I would talk to my warders
freely and friendly and clearly,
as though it were mine to command.

Who am I? They also tell me
I would bear the days of misfortune
equally, smilingly, proudly,
like one accustomed to win.

Am I then really all that which other men tell of?
Or am I only what I know of myself?
restless and longing and sick, like a bird in a cage,
struggling for breath, as though hands were compressing my throat,
yearning for colors, for flowers, for the voices of birds,
thirsting for words of kindness, for neighborliness,
trembling with anger at despotisms and petty humiliation,
tossing in expectation of great events,
powerlessly trembling for friends at an infinite distance,
weary and empty at praying, at thinking, at making,
faint, and ready to say farewell to it all?

Who am I? This or the other?
Am I one person today and tomorrow another?
Am I both at once? A hypocrite before others,
and before myself a contemptible woebegone weakling?
Or is something within me still like a beaten army,
fleeing in disorder from victory already achieved?

Who am I? They mock me, these lonely questions of mine.
Whoever I am, Thou knowest, O God, I am thine.

What does it mean to be created for a special purpose?

Look at the things around you. What are they? (For example, is there a pen, journal, soft drink bottle, bedspread, chair, lamp, or window?)

Each of those things has been created for a specific purpose. God created you with much more care and thoughtfulness than the maker of your lamp or window or pen put into making those objects. If you are so special to God, how do you think God wants to use you?

The catechism says this:

> **Question 1.** *What is God's purpose for your life?*
> God wills that I should live by the grace of the Lord Jesus Christ, for the love of God, and in the communion of the Holy Spirit.

What specific things do you think God "wills" for your life that might be different than what God wills for someone else's life?

What special gifts or talents have you been given to use for God's purpose?

How can you practice putting those gifts to work this week?

looking ahead

Read the key catechism questions for our next group session slowly. Is there one sentence or phrase that sticks with you?

Question 25. *What do you believe when you confess your faith in Jesus Christ as "God's only Son"?*

No one else will ever be God incarnate. No one else will ever die for the sins of the world. Only Jesus Christ is such a person, only he could do such a work, and he in fact has done it.

Question 26. *What do you affirm when you confess your faith in Jesus Christ as "our Lord"?*

That having been raised from the dead Christ reigns with compassion and justice over all things in heaven and on earth, especially over those who confess him by faith. By loving and serving him above all else, I give glory and honor to God.

Question 30. *What is the significance of affirming that Jesus is truly God?*

Only God properly can deserve worship. Only God can reveal to us who God is. And only God can save us from our sins. Being truly God, Jesus meets these conditions. He is the proper object of our worship, the self-revelation of God, and the Savior of the world.

Question 31. *What is the significance of affirming that Jesus is also truly a human being?*

Being truly human, Jesus entered fully into our fallen situation and overcame it. He lived a life of pure obedience to God, even to the point of accepting a violent death. When we accept him by faith, he removes our disobedience and clothes us with his perfect righteousness.

Question 33. *What do you affirm when you say that he was "crucified, dead, and buried"?*

From Christ's lonely and terrible death, we learn that there is no sorrow he has not known, no grief he has not borne, and no price he was unwilling to pay in order to reconcile us to God.

Did you find a sentence or phrase that stuck with you?

Here are some ideas. . . .

By loving and serving him above all else, I give glory and honor to God.
Only God properly can deserve worship. Only God can reveal to us who God is.
And only God can save us from our sins. Being truly God, Jesus meets these conditions.
Jesus entered fully into our fallen situation and overcame it.
and no price he was unwilling to pay in order to reconcile us to God.
No one else will ever be God incarnate. No one else will ever die for the sins of the world.

Maybe one of those, or another phrase, is particularly meaningful to you. See if you can memorize it or at least remember the gist of it.

living it out

As you go through the week, see if you can find some way that the phrase or thought or sentence you selected is lived out in the world around you. Maybe you'll see something that reminds you of it in a TV show, a magazine ad, an article from a newspaper, a conversation, or a scene from a movie. Keep some notes in the space below of how you see your phrase connecting with the world around you.

food for the soul

God, of your goodness, give me yourself: for you are sufficient for me. I cannot properly ask anything less, to be worthy of you. If I were to ask less, I should always be in want. In you alone do I have all.

—Julian of Norwich (1342–1416)

> O gracious and holy Father,
> Give us wisdom to perceive you,
> intelligence to understand you,
> diligence to seek you,
> patience to wait for you,
> eyes to see you,
> a heart to meditate on you,
> and a life to proclaim you,
> through the power of the Spirit
> of Jesus Christ our Lord.
> —St. Benedict (480–547)

Keep open—oh, keep open my eyes, my mind, my heart.

—Hermann Hagedorn

Be patient toward all that is unsolved in your heart and try to love the questions themselves, like locked rooms and like books that are now written in a very foreign tongue. Do not now seek the answers, which cannot be given to you because you would not be able to live them. And the point is, to live everything. Live the questions now. Perhaps you will then gradually, without noticing it, live along some distant day into the answer.

—Rainer Maria Rilke

... it may be that there is someone who loves you so deeply that you dare to believe that you are worth loving & so you can believe that God's love for you could be possible after all. ...

—Mother Frances Dominica

"I am not made for perilous quests," cried Frodo. "I wish I had never seen the Ring! Why did it come to me? Why was I chosen?"
"Such questions cannot be answered," said Gandalf. "You may be sure that it was not for any merit that others do not possess; not for power or wisdom, at any rate. But you have been chosen and you must therefore use such strength and heart and wits as you have."

—J. R. R. Tolkein, The Hobbit

what would you say?

WHO IS JESUS CHRIST?

the catechism

The key questions for this session are highlighted.

Question 24. *What is the second article of the Apostles' Creed?*
"And I believe in Jesus Christ, his only Son, our Lord. He was conceived by the Holy Spirit, born of the Virgin Mary, suffered under Pontius Pilate, was crucified, dead, and buried. He descended into hell. On the third day he rose again from the dead. He ascended into heaven and is seated at the right hand of the Father. He will come again to judge the living and the dead."

Question 25. *What do you believe when you confess your faith in Jesus Christ as "God's only Son"?*
No one else will ever be God incarnate. No one else will ever die for the sins of the world. Only Jesus Christ is such a person, only he could do such a work, and he in fact has done it.

Question 26. *What do you affirm when you confess your faith in Jesus Christ as "our Lord"?*
That having been raised from the dead Christ reigns with compassion and justice over all things in heaven and on earth, especially over those who confess him by faith. By loving and serving him above all else, I give glory and honor to God.

Question 27. *How did the coming of Jesus confirm God's covenant with Israel?*
God made a covenant with Israel, promising that God would be their God, that they would be God's people, and that through them all the peoples of the earth would be blessed. With the coming of Jesus the covenant was thrown open to the world. By faith in him, all peoples were welcomed into the covenant. This throwing open of the gates confirmed the promise that through Israel God's blessing would come to all.

Question 28. *Was the covenant with Israel an everlasting covenant?*

Yes. Although for the most part Israel has not accepted Jesus as the Messiah, God has not rejected Israel. God still loves Israel, and God is their hope, "for the gifts and the calling of God are irrevocable" (Rom. 11:29).

Question 29. *What do you affirm when you say he was "conceived by the Holy Spirit and born of the Virgin Mary"?*

First, that being born of Mary, Jesus was truly a human being. Second, that our Lord's incarnation was a holy and mysterious event. Third, that he was set apart by his unique origin for the sake of accomplishing our salvation.

Question 30. *What is the significance of affirming that Jesus is truly God?*

Only God can properly deserve worship. Only God can reveal to us who God is. And only God can save us from our sins. Being truly God, Jesus meets these conditions. He is the proper object of our worship, the self-revelation of God, and the Savior of the world.

Question 31. *What is the significance of affirming that Jesus is also truly a human being?*

Being truly human, Jesus entered fully into our fallen situation and overcame it. He lived a life of pure obedience to God, even to the point of accepting a violent death. When we accept him by faith, he removes our disobedience and clothes us with his perfect righteousness.

Question 32. *What do you affirm when you say that he "suffered under Pontius Pilate"?*

First, that our Lord was rejected and abused by the authorities of that time, both religious and political. Second, and even more importantly, that he submitted to condemnation by an earthly judge so that we might be acquitted before our heavenly judge.

Question 33. *What do you affirm when you say that he was "crucified, dead, and buried"?*

From Christ's lonely and terrible death we learn that there is no sorrow he has not known, no grief he has not borne, and no price he was unwilling to pay in order to reconcile us to God.

Question 34. *What do you affirm when you say that he "descended into hell"?*

That our Lord took upon himself the full consequences of our sinfulness in order that we might be spared.

Question 35. *What do you affirm when you say that "on the third day he rose again from the dead"?*

Our Lord could not be held by the power of death. Having died on the cross, he appeared to his followers and revealed himself to them as the Lord and Savior of the world.

Question 36. *What do you affirm when you say that "he ascended into heaven and is seated at the right hand of the Father"?*

First, that Christ has gone to be with his loving Father so that he is now hidden except to the eyes of faith. Second, however, that he is not cut off from us but is present here and now by grace. He reigns with divine authority, protecting us, guiding us, and interceding for us until he returns in glory.

Question 37. *How do you understand the words that "he will come again to judge the living and the dead"?*

Like everyone else, I too must stand in fear and trembling before the judgment seat of Christ. But the Judge is the one who submitted to judgment for my sake. Nothing will be able to separate me from the love of God in Christ Jesus my Lord.

reflections

The Apostles' Creed

I believe in God, the Father almighty, creator of heaven and earth.

I believe in Jesus Christ, God's only Son, our Lord, who was conceived by the Holy Spirit, born of the Virgin Mary, suffered under Pontius Pilate, was crucified, died, and was buried; he descended to the dead. On the third day he rose again; he ascended into heaven, he is seated at the right hand of the Father, and he will come to judge the living and the dead.

I believe in the Holy Spirit, the holy catholic Church, the communion of saints, the forgiveness of sins, the resurrection of the body, and the life everlasting. Amen.

Reflecting on the Apostles' Creed

Read through the following catechism questions, key points, and scripture passages. Reflect on each question and write your thoughts in the space provided.

Question 25. *What do you believe when you confess your faith in Jesus Christ as "God's only Son"?*

No one else will ever be God incarnate. No one else will ever die for the sins of the world. Only Jesus Christ is such a person, only he could do such a work, and he in fact has done it.

Question 26. *What do you affirm when you confess your faith in Jesus Christ as "our Lord"?*

That having been raised from the dead Christ reigns with compassion and justice over all things in heaven and on earth, especially those who confess him by faith. By loving and serving him above all else, I give glory and honor to God.

What does it mean that Jesus is Lord? That he "reigns"?

Do you ever feel as though something else reigns in your life?

What are some of the things that compete with God for first place in your life? Everyone can be tempted to put other things before God. For some, it is money, power, or prestige. For others, the focus is on acquiring material things like a certain car or a big house. Others want to be the center of attention and be noticed, through achievement in sports or school. Some wear clothes that make them look like they fit in with a certain crowd of friends.

What are some of the ways that we might demonstrate our love of the true God more than the false gods in life?

What are some of the ways that we are serving God? How might this activity increase in your life?

What does it mean to you to give "glory and honor" to God? Do you know anyone who you think does this?

Question 30. *What is the significance of affirming that Jesus is truly God?*

Only God properly can deserve worship. Only God can reveal to us who God is. And only God can save us from our sins. Being truly God, Jesus meets these conditions. He is the proper object of our worship, the self-revelation of God, and the Savior of the world.

Question 31. *What is the significance of affirming that Jesus is also truly a human being?*

Being truly human, Jesus entered fully into our fallen situation and overcame it. He lived a life of pure obedience to God, even to the point of accepting a violent death. When we accept him by faith, he removes our disobedience and clothes us with his perfect righteousness.

What do you think about Jesus being both God and human?

Which is it harder for you to imagine—God becoming a human being or a human being living life in perfect unity with God?

Do you think that Jesus actually suffered on the cross?

Question 33. *What do you affirm when you say that he was "crucified, dead, and buried"?*

From Christ's lonely and terrible death, we learn that there is no sorrow he has not known, no grief he has not borne, and no price he was unwilling to pay in order to reconcile us to God.

Christ knows fully what it is like to be human, even to experience loss and heartache. He stepped in and followed through on God's plan of creating a pathway to heaven through Christ's death. Christ did for us what we cannot do for ourselves.

What is a lonely place in your life right now?

How could you welcome the companionship of Christ into this area?

WWJD

We've all seen this acronym—it stands for "What Would Jesus Do?" But it could also stand for "Walk With Jesus Daily." Think about that for a minute. What would that look like?

Close your eyes and talk out loud about a typical day . . . get up, shower, eat breakfast, jump in the car to drive to school, hunt for a close parking space, run to class . . . lunchroom . . . gym . . . giving a cute girl/guy a ride home . . . homework, job, sports practice, dinner. . . .

Now, imagine that whole scenario as if you had a friend visiting you—or your cousin from out of town, maybe—who was going to tag along with you. No matter what you do, that person will be with you—on a date, in the shower, taking out the trash, putting gas in the car, going to band practice.

Now, imagine that person is Jesus. Would you do anything differently than what you're doing now? What would it be like to have Jesus tag along with you all day?

Consider Jesus Christ as your daily companion this week. Are there things that you are proud for Him to see about you?

Are there areas of your life that you hope He will not notice?

What words do you use that you hope he doesn't hear?

What things do you say or do that would have been better left unsaid or undone?

What relationships are the farthest from the way Jesus would want them?

How do you spend your free time?

How might Jesus want you to change the way you spend your free time?

looking ahead

Question 62. *What do you mean when you speak of "the forgiveness of sins"?*

Because of Jesus Christ, God no longer holds my sins against me. Christ alone is my righteousness and my life. Grace alone is the basis on which God has forgiven me in him. Faith alone is the means by which I receive Christ into my heart, and with him the forgiveness that makes me whole.

living it out

As you go through your week, look for acts and examples of forgiveness that you see around you!

food for the soul

An old rabbi was once asked why so few people were finding God. He wisely replied that people are not willing to look that low. Jesus was born in a stable, and God is especially concerned for the poorest, the lowliest, the lost, and the neglected.

—*Harvey & Lois Seifert, from* Liberation of Life

What does it mean then, to allow Jesus to be the Lord of our lives? What does it mean that anything is the lord of our life? Just this: whatever controls us is our lord. The person who seeks power is controlled by power. The person who seeks acceptance is controlled by the people he or she wants to please. We do not control ourselves. We are controlled by the lord of our life. If Jesus is our Lord, then he is the one who controls, he has the ultimate power. There are no bargains. We cannot manipulate him by playing "let's make a deal." If he is Lord, the only option open to us is to do his will, to let him have control. Jesus remains Lord whether we accept him or not. His lordship, his essence is not affected by what we choose. But our lives are drastically changed by our choice. . . .

Jesus always preserves our freedom. He allows us to choose him over all others. Jesus will not control us in the wrong way. Nor will he control us in the easy way, by making every decision for us. He controls us in the right way: by being who he is without compromise and by insisting we become all that we are meant to be. And he tells us this can occur only through following him, obeying him and maintaining a living, passionate stormy kinship to him.

—*from* Out of the Saltshaker and Into the World, *Rebecca Manley Pippert*

sin & forgiveness

WHAT DOES GOD EXPECT OF ME?

the catechism

All of the questions this week are key questions.

Question 20. *Was the image of God lost when we turned from God by falling into sin?*

Yes and no. Sin means that all our relations with others have become distorted and confused. Although we did not cease to be *with* God, our fellow human beings, and other creatures, we did cease to be *for* them; and although we did not lose our distinctive human capacities *completely*, we did lose the ability to use them *rightly*, especially in relation to God. Having ruined our connection with God by disobeying God's will, we are persons with hearts curved in upon ourselves. We have become slaves to the sin of which we are guilty, helpless to save ourselves, and are free, so far as freedom remains, only within the bounds of sin.

Question 62. *What do you mean when you speak of "the forgiveness of sins"?*

Because of Jesus Christ, God no longer holds my sins against me. Christ alone is my righteousness and my life. Grace alone is the basis on which God has forgiven me in him. Faith alone is the means by which I receive Christ into my heart, and with him the forgiveness that makes me whole.

Question 63. *Does forgiveness mean that God excuses sin?*

No. God does not cease to be God. Although God is merciful to the sinner, God does not excuse the evil of sin. For to forgive is not to excuse.

Question 64. *Does your forgiveness of those who have harmed you depend on their repentance?*

No. I am to forgive as I have been forgiven. Just as God's forgiveness of me does not depend on my first confessing and repenting of my sins, so my forgiveness of those who harm me does not depend on their doing so. However, when I forgive the person who has harmed me, I do not deny or excuse the harm that was done.

reflections

It's easy for us to see the sin in other people's lives, but we're not usually as quick to identify the sins in our own lives. Why is that?

Is it hard for you to believe that God can forgive your sins?

Read *"Repentance"* from Kathleen Norris's *Amazing Grace: A Vocabulary of Faith:*

> Children who are picked on by their big brothers and sisters can be remarkably adept when it comes to writing cursing psalms, and I believe that the writing process offers them a safe haven in which to work through their desires for vengeance in a healthy way. Once a little boy wrote a poem called, "The Monster Who Was Sorry." He began by admitting that he hates it when his father yells at him; his response in the poem is to throw his sister down the stairs, and then to wreck his room, and finally to wreck the whole town. The poem concludes: "Then I sit in my messy house and say to myself, 'I shouldn't have done all that.'" "My messy house" says it all: with more honesty than most adults could have mustered, the boy made a metaphor for himself that admitted the depth of his rage and also gave him a way out. If that boy had been a novice in the fourth-century monastic desert, the elders might have told him that he was well on the way to repentance, not such a monster after all, but only human. If the house is messy, they might have said, why not clean it up, why not make it into a place where God might wish to dwell?

Think about the sin you have chosen to confess to God.

What change will you make in your life?

What would the new approach look like?

looking ahead

Read the key catechism questions for the next group session slowly. Is there one sentence or phrase there sticks with you?

Question 38. *Will all human beings be saved?*

No one will be lost who can be saved. The limits to salvation, whatever they may be, are known only to God. Three truths above all are certain. God is a holy God who is not to be trifled with. No one will be saved except by grace alone. And no judge could possibly be more gracious than our Lord and Savior, Jesus Christ.

Question 43. *What do you believe when you confess your faith in the Holy Spirit?*

The Holy Spirit is the divine person who enables us to love, know, and serve Jesus Christ.

Question 45. *What do you mean when you speak of "the Word of God"?*

"Jesus Christ as he is attested for us in Holy Scripture is the one Word of God whom we have to hear, and whom we have to trust and obey in life and in death" (Barmen Declaration, Article I).

Question 46. *Isn't Holy Scripture also the Word of God?*

Yes. Holy Scripture is also God's Word because of its focus, its function, and its founder. Its central focus is Jesus Christ, the living Word. Its basic function is to deepen our love, knowledge, and service of him as our Savior and Lord. And its dependable founder is the Holy Spirit, who spoke through the prophets and apostles, and who inspires us with eager desire for the truths that Scripture contains.

Did you find a sentence or phrase to hang on to?

Here are some ideas. . . .

No one will be lost who can be saved.

The Holy Spirit is the divine person who enables us to love, know, and serve Jesus Christ.

God is a holy God who is not to be trifled with.

Maybe one of these, or another phrase, is particularly meaningful to you. See if you can memorize it, or at least remember the gist of it.

living it out

As you go through the week, see if you can find some way that the phrase or sentence you selected is lived out in the world around you. Maybe you'll see something that reminds you of it in a TV show, a magazine ad, an article from a newspaper, a conversation, or a scene from a movie. Keep some notes in the space below of how you see your phrase connecting with the world around you.

food for the soul

We love you, O our God; and we desire to love you more and more. Grant to us that we may love you as much as we desire, and as much as we ought. O dearest friend, who has so loved and saved us, the thought of whom is so sweet and always growing sweeter, come with Christ and dwell in our heart; then you will keep a watch over our lips, our steps, our deeds, and we shall not need to be anxious either for our souls or our bodies. Give us love, sweetest of all gifts, which knows no enemy. Give us in our hearts pure love, born of your love to us, that we may love others as you love us. O most loving Father of Jesus Christ, from whom flows all love, let our hearts, frozen in sin, cold to you and cold to others, be warmed by this divine fire. So help and bless us in your Son. Amen.

—*St. Anselm, Archbishop of Canterbury (1033–1109)*

See, Lord, an empty vessel that needs to be filled. My Lord, fill it. I am weak in the faith; strengthen me. I am cold in love; warm me and make me fervent so that my love may go out to my neighbor. I do not have a strong and firm faith; at times I doubt and am unable to trust you altogether. O Lord, help me. Strengthen my faith and trust in you. In you I have sealed all the treasures I have. I am poor; you are rich and came to be merciful to the poor. I am a sinner; you are upright. With me there is an abundance of sin; in you is the fullness of righteousness. Therefore, I will remain with you from whom I can receive, but to whom I may not give.

—*Martin Luther (1483–1546)*

the Holy Spirit and a relationship with Christ

HOW CAN I KNOW GOD?

the catechism

The key questions for this session are highlighted.

Question 36. What do you affirm when you say that "he ascended into heaven and is seated at the right hand of the Father"?
First, that Christ has gone to be with his loving Father so that he is now hidden except to the eyes of faith. Second, however, that he is not cut off from us but is present here and now by grace. He reigns with divine authority, protecting us, guiding us, and interceding for us until he returns in glory.

Question 37. How do you understand the words that "he will come again to Judge the living and the dead"?
Like everyone else, I too must stand in fear and trembling before the judgment seat of Christ. But the Judge is the one who submitted to judgment for my sake. Nothing will be able to separate me from the love of God in Christ Jesus my Lord.

Question 38. Will all human beings be saved?
No one will be lost who can be saved. The limits to salvation, whatever they may be, are known only to God. Three truths above all are certain. God is a holy God who is not to be trifled with. No one will be saved except by grace alone. And no judge could possibly be more gracious than our Lord and Savior, Jesus Christ.

Question 39. How should I treat non-Christians and people of other religions?
I should meet friendship with friendship, hostility with kindness, generosity with gratitude, persecution with forbearance, truth with agreement, and error with truth. I should express my faith by word and by deed. I should avoid compromising the truth on the one hand and being narrow-minded on the other. In short, I should welcome and accept these others in a way that honors and reflects the Lord's welcome and acceptance of me.

Question 40. *How will God deal with the followers of other religions?*

God offers salvation to all human beings through Jesus Christ. How God will deal with those who do not know or follow Christ, but who follow another tradition, we cannot finally say. We can say, however, that God is gracious and merciful, and that God will not deal with people in any other way than we see in Jesus Christ, who came as the Savior of the world.

Question 41. *Is Christianity the only true religion?*

By the grace of God, Christianity offers the truth of the gospel. Although other religions may contain various truths, no other can or does affirm the name of Jesus Christ as the hope of the world.

Question 42. *What is the third article of the Apostles' Creed?*

"I believe in the Holy Spirit, the holy catholic church, the communion of saints, the forgiveness of sins, the resurrection of the body, and the life everlasting. Amen."

Question 43. *What do you believe when you confess your faith in the Holy Spirit?*

The Holy Spirit is the divine person who enables us to love, know, and serve Jesus Christ.

Question 44. *How do we receive the Holy Spirit?*

By receiving the Word of God. The Spirit arrives with the Word, brings us to rebirth, and assures us of eternal life. The Spirit nurtures, corrects, and strengthens us with the truth of the Word.

Question 45. *What do you mean when you speak of "the Word of God"?*

"Jesus Christ as he is attested for us in Holy Scripture is the one Word of God whom we have to hear, and whom we have to trust and obey in life and in death" (Barmen Declaration, Article I).

Question 46. *Isn't Holy Scripture also the Word of God?*

Yes. Holy Scripture is also God's Word because of its focus, its function, and its founder. Its central focus is Jesus Christ, the living Word. Its basic function is to deepen our love, knowledge, and service of him as our Savior and Lord. And its dependable founder is the Holy Spirit, who spoke through the prophets and apostles, and who inspires us with eager desire for the truths that Scripture contains.

Question 47. *Isn't preaching also the Word of God?*

Yes. Preaching is God's Word when it is faithful to the witness of Holy Scripture. Faith comes by hearing God's Word in the form of faithful preaching and teaching.

reflections

ASSESSING YOUR SPIRITUAL LIFE

The Spirit-led process of growing in Christ is called sanctification. If your spiritual life were to be assessed in the same way that a doctor does an annual physical or a teacher gives a quarterly report card, which areas are strongest and which need increased attention?

> Loving God,
>
> knowing God,
>
> serving Christ?

This week, think about how the Spirit works in you.

APPLAUSE FOR OTHERS

Think of a time when you applauded someone else. What did he or she do that made you want to cheer him or her on?

Are there ways that you could be a better fan, encouraging your friends or family in their pursuits?

PRAISE OR APPLAUSE

Who or what lifts your spirit? Who praises or applauds you and how does he or she do it?

looking ahead

Question 49. *What is the mission of the church?*

The mission of the church is to bear witness to God's love for the world in Jesus Christ.

Question 52. *What do you affirm when you speak of "the communion of saints"?*

All those who live in union with Christ, whether on earth or with God in heaven, are "saints." Our communion with Christ makes us members one of another. The ties that bind us in Christ are deeper than any other human relationship.

living it out

This week, ask three people (at least one of whom is not a member of your congregation) to answer the following questions:

What's the first thing that comes into your mind when you hear the word "church"?

How would you define church?

Think about different things the church has meant to you at different times in your life.

food for the soul

If then, you suffer from moral anemia, take my advice and steer clear of Christianity. If you want to live a life of easy-going self-indulgence, whatever you do, do not become a Christian. But if you want a life of self-discovery, deeply satisfying to the nature God has given you; if you want a life of adventure in which you have the privilege of serving God and others; if you want a life in which to express something of the overwhelming gratitude you are beginning to feel for him who died for you, then I would urge you to yield your life, without reserve and without delay, to your Lord and Saviour, Jesus Christ.

—*John R.W. Stott,* Basic Christianity

> Christ, be with me, Christ before me, Christ behind me,
> Christ in me, Christ beneath me, Christ above me,
> Christ on my right, Christ on my left,
> Christ where I lie, Christ where I sit, Christ where I arise,
> Christ in the heart of every one who thinks of me,
> Christ in every eye that sees me,
> Christ in every ear that hears me.
> Salvation is of the Lord,
> Salvation is of the Christ,
> May your salvation, O Lord, be ever with us.
>
> —*St. Patrick of Ireland*

Come and help us, Lord Jesus. A vision of your face will brighten us; but to feel your spirit touching us will make us vigorous. Oh! for the leaping and walking of the man born lame. May we today dance with holy joy, like David before the ark of God. May a holy exhilaration take possession of every part of us; may we be glad in the Lord; may our mouth be filled with laughter, and our tongue with singing, "for the Lord hath done great things for us whereof we are glad."

—*C.H. Spurgeon (1834–1892)*

We are all meant to be God-bearers. What good is it to me if this eternal birth of the divine Son takes place unceasingly but does not take place within myself? And, what good is it to me if Mary is full of grace if I am not also full of grace? What good is it to me for the Creator to give birth to his Son if I do not also give birth to him in my time and my culture? This, then is the fullness of time: when the Son of God is begotten in us.

—*Meister Eckhart*

the church & its mission

IF GOD SLEPT IN ON SUNDAYS, WHY CAN'T I?

the catechism

The key questions for this session are highlighted.

Question 48. *What do you affirm when you speak of "the holy catholic church"?*

The church is the community of all faithful people who have given their lives to Jesus Christ with thanksgiving. The church is holy because he is holy, and universal (or "catholic") in significance because he is universal in significance. Despite all its remaining imperfections here and now, the church is called to become ever more holy and catholic, for that is what it already is in Christ.

Question 49. *What is the mission of the church?*

The mission of the church is to bear witness to God's love for the world in Jesus Christ.

Question 50. *What forms does this mission take?*

The church's mission takes a wide variety of forms, including evangelism, work for social justice, and ministries of care. Yet the center is always the same: Jesus Christ. In every case the church extends mercy and forgiveness to the needy in a way that points finally to him.

Question 51. *Who are the needy?*

The hungry need bread, the homeless need a roof, the oppressed need justice, and the lonely need fellowship. At the same time—on another and deeper level—the hopeless need hope, sinners need forgiveness, and the world needs the gospel. On this level no one is excluded, and all the needy are one. Our mission as the church is to bring hope to a desperate world by declaring God's undying love—as one beggar tells another where to find bread.

Question 52. *What do you affirm when you speak of "the communion of saints"?*

All those who live in union with Christ, whether on earth or with God in heaven, are "saints." Our communion with Christ makes us members one of another. The ties that bind us in Christ are deeper than any other human relationship.

reflections

Have you ever thought of yourself as a saint?

What "saintly" qualities do you have?

How could you use those to serve Jesus Christ and the world?

What has the church meant to you at different times in your life?

How have you seen your congregation "bear witness to God's love for the world in Jesus Christ"?

looking ahead

Read through the key questions for the next group session carefully. Choose a phrase or sentence to hang on to for the week.

Question 53. *How do you enter into communion with Christ and so with one another?*

By the power of the Holy Spirit as it works through Word and sacrament. The Scriptures acknowledge two sacraments as instituted by our Lord Jesus Christ—baptism and the Lord's Supper.

Question 54. *What is a sacrament?*

A sacrament is a special act of Christian worship, instituted by Christ, which uses a visible sign to proclaim the promise of the gospel for the forgiveness of sins and eternal life. In baptism the sign is that of water; in the Lord's Supper, that of bread and wine.

Question 56. *What does it mean to be baptized?*

My baptism means that I am joined to Jesus Christ forever. As I am baptized with water, he baptizes me with his Spirit, washing away all my sins and freeing me from their control. My baptism is a sign that one day I will rise with him in glory, and may walk with him even now in newness of life.

Question 61. *What does it mean to share in the Lord's Supper?*

When we celebrate the Lord's Supper, the Lord Jesus Christ is truly present, pouring out his Spirit upon us. By his Spirit, the bread that we break and the cup that we bless share in his body and blood. As I receive the bread and the cup, remembering that Christ died even for me, I feed on him in my heart by faith with thanksgiving. His life becomes mine, and my life becomes his, to all eternity.

SACRAMENT SEARCH AT HOME

Baptism

Have you been baptized?

If so, do you remember anything about it?

Ask your parents, grandparents, or a family friend if they can tell you anything about your baptism. When did it happen? How old were you? Who was there? Did anything special occur?

If you've never been baptized, why do you suppose that is? Many people choose not to be baptized until they are adults. What would be their reason for that?

Lord's Supper

How often does your church celebrate the Lord's Supper?

Do you wish it happened more or less frequently?

Think of a time when the Lord's Supper (Communion) was particularly meaningful for you. When was that? Why was it so meaningful?

food for the soul

I don't know what your destiny will be, but one thing I do know: the only ones among you who will be really happy are those who have sought and found how to serve.

—*Albert Schweitzer*

Lord, open our eyes,
That we may see you in our brothers and sisters.
Lord, open our ears,
That we may hear the cries of the hungry, the cold,
the frightened, the oppressed.
Lord, open our hearts,
That we may love each other as you love us.
Renew in us your spirit
Lord, free us and make us one.

—*Mother Teresa of Calcutta*

The Church is in the world to save the world. It is a tool of God for that purpose; not a comfortable religious club established in fine historical premises. Every one of its members is required, in one way or another, to cooperate with the Spirit in working for that great end: and much of this work will be done in secret and invisible ways. We are transmitters as well as receivers. Our contemplation and our action, our humble self-opening to God, keeping ourselves sensitive to God's music and light, and our generous self-opening to our fellow creatures, keeping ourselves sensitive to their needs, ought to form one's life; meditating between God and God's world, and bringing the saving power of the Eternal into time.

—*Evelyn Underhill,* The Spiritual Life

the sacraments and the lord's prayer

THE CHURCH'S TOOLBOX

the catechism

The key questions for this session are highlighted.

Question 53. *How do you enter into communion with Christ and so with one another?*

By the power of the Holy Spirit as it works through Word and sacrament. The Scriptures acknowledge two sacraments as instituted by our Lord Jesus Christ—baptism and the Lord's Supper.

Question 54. *What is a sacrament?*

A sacrament is a special act of Christian worship, instituted by Christ, which uses a visible sign to proclaim the promise of the gospel for the forgiveness of sins and eternal life. In baptism the sign is that of water; in the Lord's Supper, that of bread and wine.

Question 55. *What is baptism?*

Baptism is the sign and seal through which we are joined to Christ.

Question 56. *What does it mean to be baptized?*

My baptism means that I am joined to Jesus Christ forever. As I am baptized with water, he baptizes me with his Spirit, washing away all my sins and freeing me from their control. My baptism is a sign that one day I will rise with him in glory, and may walk with him even now in newness of life.

Question 57. *Are infants also to be baptized?*

Yes. Along with their believing parents, they are included in the great hope of the gospel and belong to the people of God. Forgiveness and faith are both promised to them through Christ's covenant with his people.

Question 58. *Why are you baptized in the name of the Father, and of the Son, and of the Holy Spirit?*

Because of the command Jesus gave his disciples. After he was raised from the dead, he appeared to them and said, "Go therefore and make disciples of all nations, baptizing them in the name of the Father and of the Son and of the Holy Spirit" (Matt. 28:19).

Question 59. *What is the meaning of this name?*

It is the name of the Holy Trinity. The Father is God, the Son is God, and the Holy Spirit is God. And yet they are not three gods, but one God in three persons. We worship God in this mystery.

Question 60. *What is the Lord's Supper?*

The Lord's Supper is the sign and seal by which our communion with Christ is renewed.

Question 61. *What does it mean to share in the Lord's Supper?*

When we celebrate the Lord's Supper, the Lord Jesus Christ is truly present, pouring out his Spirit upon us. By his Spirit, the bread that we break and the cup that we bless share in his body and blood. As I receive the bread and the cup, remembering that Christ died even for me, I feed on him in my heart by faith with thanksgiving. His life becomes mine, and my life becomes his, to all eternity.

Question 97. *What prayer serves as our rule or pattern?*

Our rule or pattern is found in the Lord's Prayer, which Jesus taught to his disciples:

> *Our Father in heaven,*
> *hallowed be your name,*
> *your kingdom come,*
> *your will be done,*
> *on earth as in heaven.*
> *Give us today our daily bread.*
> *Forgive us our sins*
> *as we forgive those who sin against us.*
> *Save us from the time of trial*
> *and deliver us from evil.*
> *For the kingdom, the power, and the glory are yours*
> *now and for ever. Amen.*

These words express everything that we may desire and expect from God.

Question 98. *What is meant by addressing God as "Our Father in heaven"?*

When we pray to God as "our Father in heaven," we draw near with childlike reverence and place ourselves securely in God's hands. We express our confidence that God cares for us, and that nothing on earth is beyond the reach of God's grace.

Question 99. *What is meant by the first petition, "Hallowed be your name"?*

This petition is placed first, because it expresses the goal and purpose of the whole prayer. When we pray for God's name to be "hallowed," we ask that we will know and glorify God as God really is, and that all things will truly come to serve God.

Question 100. *What is meant by the second petition, "Your kingdom come"?*

We ask God to come and rule among us through faith, love, and justice. We pray for both the church and the world, that God will rule in our hearts through faith, in our personal relationships through love, and in our institutional affairs through justice.

Question 101. *What is meant by the third petition, "Your will be done, on earth as in heaven"?*

Of course, God's will is always done and will surely come to pass, whether we desire it or not. But the phrase "on earth as in heaven" means that we ask for the grace to do God's will on earth in the way that it is done in heaven—gladly and from the heart. We yield ourselves, in life and in death, to God's will.

Question 102. *What is meant by the fourth petition, "Give us today our daily bread"?*

We ask God to supply all our needs, for we know that God, who cares for us in every area of our life, has promised to give us temporal as well as spiritual blessings. God commands us to pray each day for all that we need and no more, so that we will learn to rely completely on God.

Question 103. *What is meant by the fifth petition, "Forgive us our sins as we forgive those who sin against us"?*

We pray that a new and right spirit will be put within us. We ask for the grace to treat others with the same mercy we have received from God. We ask that we will not resent or strike back at those who harm us, but that our hearts will be knit together with the merciful heart of God.

Question 104. *What is meant by the final petition, "Save us from the time of trial and deliver us from evil"?*

We ask God to protect us from all that threatens to hurt or destroy us. We pray for the ability to resist sin and evil in our own lives, and for the grace to endure suffering in trust and without bitterness when it is unavoidable. We ask for the grace to believe in the love of God that will finally swallow up all the evil and hatred in the world.

Question 105. *What is meant by the closing doxology, "For the kingdom, the power, and the glory are yours now and for ever"?*

We give God thanks and praise for the kingdom more powerful than all enemies, for the power perfected in the weakness of love, and for the glory that includes our well-being and that of the whole creation, both now and to all eternity.

Question 106. *What is meant by the word "Amen"?*

"Amen" means "so be it" or "let it be so." It expresses our complete confidence in the triune God, the God of the covenant with Israel as fulfilled through our Lord Jesus Christ, who makes no promise that will not be kept, and whose mercy endures forever.

reflections

Think of a time when you felt close to God or sensed God's presence with you. Where were you? What was it like?

Have you ever sensed God's presence with you while you were praying or while you were worshiping?

Is it hard or easy for you to talk to God?

How do you talk to God? Out loud? In a journal? Silently? While you're exercising or when you're waking up?

Does the Lord's Prayer help you to know how it is that we can talk to God?

looking ahead

Read through the catechism questions for the next group session carefully. The key questions for that session are highlighted.

Question 65. *What do you mean when you speak of "the resurrection of the body"?*

Because Christ lives, we will live also. Death is not the end of human life. The whole person, body and soul, will be raised from death to eternal life with God.

Question 66. *What do you affirm when you speak of "the life everlasting"?*

God does not will to be God without us, but instead grants to us creatures—fallen and mortal as we are—eternal life. Communion with Jesus Christ is eternal life itself.

Question 67. *Won't heaven be a boring place?*

No. Heaven is our true home, a world of love. There we shall at last see face to face what we now only glimpse as through a distant mirror. Our deepest, truest delights in this life are only a dim foreshadowing of the delights that await us in heaven.

II. THE TEN COMMANDMENTS

Question 68. *What are the Ten Commandments?*

The Ten Commandments give a summary of God's law for our lives. They teach us how to live rightly with God and one another.

Question 69. *Why should you obey this law?*

Not to win God's love, for God already loves me. Not to earn my salvation, for Christ has earned it for me. Not to avoid being punished, for then I would obey out of fear. With gladness in my heart I should obey God's law out of gratitude, for God has blessed me by it and given it for my well-being.

Question 70. *What is the first commandment?*
You shall have no other gods before me (Ex. 20:3; Deut. 5:7).

Question 71. *What do you learn from this commandment?*
No loyalty comes before my loyalty to God. I should worship and serve only God, expect all good from God alone, and love, fear, and honor God with all my heart.

Question 72. *What is the second commandment?*
You shall not make for yourself an idol (Ex. 20:4; Deut. 5:8).

Question 73. *What do you learn from this commandment?*
First, when I treat anything other than God as though it were God, I make it an idol. Second, when I assume that my own interests are more important than anything else, I make them into idols, and in effect I also make an idol of myself.

Question 74. *What is the third commandment?*
You shall not make wrongful use of the name of the Lord your God (Ex. 20:7; Deut. 5:11).

Question 75. *What do you learn from this commandment?*
I should use God's name with reverence and awe. God's name is holy and deserves the highest honor from us. It is insulted when used carelessly, as in a curse or a pious cliché.

Question 76. *What is the fourth commandment?*
Remember the Sabbath Day, and keep it holy (Ex. 20:8; Deut. 5:12).

Question 77. *What do you learn from this commandment?*
God requires a special day to be set apart so that worship can be at the center of my life. It is right to honor God with thanks and praise, and to hear and receive God's Word.

Question 78. *What is the best summary of the first four commandments?*

These teach me how to live rightly with God. Jesus summed them up with the commandment he called the first and greatest: You shall love the Lord your God with all your heart, and with all your soul, and with all your mind (Matt. 22:37; Deut. 6:5).

Question 79. *What is the fifth commandment?*

Honor your father and your mother (Ex. 20:12; Deut. 5:16).

Question 80. *What do you learn from this commandment?*

Though I owe reverence to God alone, I owe genuine respect to my parents, both my mother and father. God wills me to listen to them, be thankful for the benefits I receive from them, and be considerate of their needs, especially in old age.

Question 81. *Are there limits to your obligation to obey them?*

Yes. No mere human being is God. Blind obedience is not required, for everything should be tested by loyalty and obedience to God.

Question 82. *What is the sixth commandment?*

You shall not murder (Ex. 20:13; Deut. 5:17).

Question 83. *What do you learn from this commandment?*

God forbids anything that harms my neighbor unfairly. Murder or injury can be done not only by direct violence but also by an angry word or a clever plan, and not only by an individual but also by unjust social institutions. I should honor every human being, including my enemy, as a person made in God's image.

Question 84. *What is the seventh commandment?*

You shall not commit adultery (Ex. 20:14; Deut. 5:18).

Question 85. *What do you learn from this commandment?*
God requires fidelity and purity in sexual relations. Since love is God's great gift, God expects me not to corrupt it, or confuse it with momentary desire or the selfish fulfillment of my own pleasures. God forbids all sexual immorality, whether in married or in single life.

Question 86. *What is the eighth commandment?*
You shall not steal (Ex. 20:15; Deut. 5:19).

Question 87. *What do you learn from this commandment?*
God forbids all theft and robbery, including schemes, tricks, or systems that unjustly take what belongs to someone else. God requires me not to be driven by greed, not to misuse or waste the gifts I have been given, and not to distrust the promise that God will supply my needs.

Question 88. *What is the ninth commandment?*
You shall not bear false witness against your neighbor (Ex. 20:16; Deut. 5:20).

Question 89. *What do you learn from this commandment?*
God forbids me to damage the honor or reputation of my neighbor. I should not say false things against anyone for the sake of money, favor, or friendship, or for the sake of revenge, or for any other reason. God requires me to speak well of my neighbor when I can, and to view the faults of my neighbor with tolerance when I cannot.

Question 90. *Does this commandment forbid racism and other forms of negative stereotyping?*
Yes. In forbidding false witness against my neighbor, God forbids me to be prejudiced against people who belong to any vulnerable, different, or disfavored social group. Jews, women, homosexuals, racial and ethnic minorities, and national enemies are among those who have suffered terribly from being subjected to the slurs of social prejudice.

Question 91. *What is the tenth commandment?*
You shall not covet what is your neighbor's (Ex. 20:17; Deut. 5:21).

Question 92. *What do you learn from this commandment?*

My whole heart should belong to God alone, not to money or the things of this world. "Coveting" means desiring something wrongfully. I should not resent the good fortune or success of my neighbor or allow envy to corrupt my heart.

Question 93. *What is the best summary of the last six commandments?*

These teach me how to live rightly with my neighbor. Jesus summed them up with a commandment which is like the greatest one about loving God: You shall love your neighbor as yourself (Matt. 22:39; Lev. 19:18).

Question 94. *Can you obey these commandments perfectly?*

No. Yet there is more grace in God than sin in me. While I must confess my sins to God and resolve not to commit them, I can be confident that God is forgiving, and will give me the grace to grow in love and knowledge day by day.

III. THE LORD'S PRAYER

Question 95. *What is prayer?*

Prayer means calling upon God whose Spirit is always present with us. In prayer we approach God with reverence, confidence, and humility. Prayer involves both addressing God in praise, confession, thanksgiving, and supplication, and listening for God's word within our hearts. When we adore God, we are filled with wonder, love, and praise before God's heavenly glory. When we confess our sins to God, we ask for forgiveness with sorry hearts. When we give thanks to God, we acknowledge God's great goodness in all that has been provided for us. Finally, when we call upon God to hear our requests, we affirm that God is always near to us in times of need and sorrow.

Question 96. *What is the purpose of prayer?*

Prayer brings us into communion with God. The more our lives are rooted in prayer, the more we sense how wonderful God is in grace, purity, majesty, and love. Prayer means offering our lives completely to God, submitting ourselves to God's will, and waiting faithfully for God's grace. Through prayer God frees us from anxiety, equips us for service, and deepens our faith.

Which of the Ten Commandments is most applicable to your life right now?

Which one is hardest to keep? Why?

Which one is easiest to keep? Why?

Read the catechism questions again, focusing on the key questions. Is there one sentence or phrase that sticks with you?

Here are some ideas:

...Yet there is more grace in God than sin in me.

...Why should you obey this law?

Not to win God's love, for God already loves me. Not to earn my salvation, for Christ has earned it for me. Not to avoid being punished, for then I would obey out of fear.

Maybe one of these, or one of the Ten Commandments, is particularly meaningful to you. See if you can memorize it, or at least remember the gist of it.

living it out

Again, as you go through the week see if you can find some way that a particular commandment shows up in the world around you. Maybe you'll see something that reminds you of it in a TV show, a magazine ad, an article from a newspaper, a conversation, or a scene from a movie. Keep notes on the connections you make between the catechism and the world you live in in the space below.

Each day this week, look for a "taste of heaven" and write or draw it here in your journal. Maybe you will notice the words of a song, a picture of caring, or a moment with your family or a friend that you want to record in your journal. How many "tastes of heaven" can you find this week?

food for the soul

On the whole, I do not find Christians, outside of the catacombs, sufficiently sensible of conditions. Does anyone have the foggiest idea what sort of power we so blithely invoke? Or, as I suspect, does no one believe a word of it? The churches are children playing on the floor with their chemistry sets, mixing up a batch of TNT to kill a Sunday morning. It is madness to wear ladies' straw hats and velvet hats to church; we should all be wearing crash helmets. Ushers should issue life preservers and signal flares; they should lash us to our pews. For the sleeping god may wake someday and take offense, or the waking god may draw us out to where we can never return.

—Annie Dillard,
from Teaching a Stone to Talk

Church is other people, a worshiping community. The worship, or praise of God, does not take place only when people gather on Sunday morning, but when they gather to paint the house of an elderly shut-in, when they visit someone in the hospital or console the bereaved, when the Sunday school kids sing Christmas carols at the nursing home. If a church has life, its "programs" are not just activity, but worship. And this is helpful, because if the Sunday morning service falls flat, it is the other forms of worship that sustain this life. When formal worship seems less than worshipful and it often does—if I am bored by the sheer weight of words in Presbyterian worship— and I often am—I have only to look around at the other people in the pews to remind myself that we are engaged in something important, something that transcends our feeble attempts at worship, and even transcends my crankiness.

Kathleen Norris, Amazing Grace:
A Vocabulary of Faith

The church is the church only when it exists for others.

—Dietrich Bonhoeffer

developing a rule of life

HOW DOES GOD EXPECT US TO LIVE?

the catechism

The key questions for this session are highlighted.

Question 79. *What is the fifth commandment?*
Honor your father and your mother (Ex. 20:12; Deut. 5:16).

Question 80. *What do you learn from this commandment?*
Though I owe reverence to God alone, I owe genuine respect to my parents, both my mother and father. God wills me to listen to them, be thankful for the benefits I receive from them, and be considerate of their needs, especially in old age.

Question 81. *Are there limits to your obligation to obey them?*
Yes. No mere human being is God. Blind obedience is not required, for everything should be tested by loyalty and obedience to God.

Question 82. *What is the sixth commandment?*
You shall not murder (Ex. 20:13; Deut. 5:17).

Question 83. *What do you learn from this commandment?*
God forbids anything that harms my neighbor unfairly. Murder or injury can be done not only by direct violence but also by an angry word or a clever plan, and not only by an individual but also by unjust social institutions. I should honor every human being, including my enemy, as a person made in God's image.

Question 84. *What is the seventh commandment?*
You shall not commit adultery (Ex. 20:14; Deut. 5:18).

Question 85. *What do you learn from this commandment?*
God requires fidelity and purity in sexual relations. Since love is God's great gift, God expects me not to corrupt it, or confuse it with momentary desire or the selfish fulfillment of my own pleasures. God forbids all sexual immorality, whether in married or in single life.

Question 86. *What is the eighth commandment?*
You shall not steal (Ex. 20:15; Deut. 5:19).

Question 87. *What do you learn from this commandment?*
God forbids all theft and robbery, including schemes, tricks, or systems that unjustly take what belongs to someone else. God requires me not to be driven by greed, not to misuse or waste the gifts I have been given, and not to distrust the promise that God will supply my needs.

Question 88. *What is the ninth commandment?*
You shall not bear false witness against your neighbor (Ex. 20:16; Deut. 5:20).

Question 89. *What do you learn from this commandment?*
God forbids me to damage the honor or reputation of my neighbor. I should not say false things against anyone for the sake of money, favor, or friendship, or for the sake of revenge, or for any other reason. God requires me to speak well of my neighbor when I can, and to view the faults of my neighbor with tolerance when I cannot.

Question 90. *Does this commandment forbid racism and other forms of negative stereotyping?*

Yes. In forbidding false witness against my neighbor, God forbids me to be prejudiced against people who belong to any vulnerable, different, or disfavored social group. Jews, women, homosexuals, racial and ethnic minorities, and national enemies are among those who have suffered terribly from being subjected to the slurs of social prejudice.

Question 91. *What is the tenth commandment?*

You shall not covet what is your neighbor's (Ex. 20:17; Deut. 5:21).

Question 92. *What do you learn from this commandment?*

My whole heart should belong to God alone, not to money or the things of this world. "Coveting" means desiring something wrongfully. I should not resent the good fortune or success of my neighbor or allow envy to corrupt my heart.

Question 93. *What is the best summary of the last six commandments?*

These teach me how to live rightly with my neighbor. Jesus summed them up with a commandment which is like the greatest one about loving God: You shall love your neighbor as yourself (Matt. 22:39; Lev. 19:18).

Question 94. *Can you obey these commandments perfectly?*

No. Yet there is more grace in God than sin in me. While I must confess my sins to God and resolve not to commit them, I can be confident that God is forgiving, and will give me the grace to grow in love and knowledge day by day.

where will you go from here?

Congratulations! You have made it through the seven sessions of *Can We Talk? Conversations for Faith*. You now have a greater understanding of our faith and how it connects with your life. Before you stash this journal under your bed or in the circular file, take a few moments to evaluate your experience and decide where you will go from here.

What did you like the most about the group sessions?

What did you find the most difficult?

What did you like about the journal? What did you find difficult about the journal?

What is one truth that you have learned in this class that you will take with you and never forget?

If asked what you believe, how would you respond?

What habits of prayer, scripture reading, reflection, and action have you developed while working in this journal? Which of those do you want to continue? What new habits would you like to try?

How have you made new friends or strengthened old friendships during the group sessions?

What steps will you take to continue to develop those relationships?

food for the soul

Our prayer for you . . .

Now may God go with you.
Above you to inspire you,
Beneath you to support you,
In front of you to lead you,
Behind you to encourage you,
Beside you to be your friend,
And within your heart,
To give you grace, and strength,
and peace.

Amen.